HOW TO PASS EXAMINATIONS

How to Pass Examinations

A down to earth guide for students aged twelve to twenty-one and their parents

by

JOHN ERASMUS

This book has been written by an examiner with long experience of academic and professional examinations. It considers the system as it is and offers guidance on the best way to prepare for and pass examinations.

FIFTH EDITION
Revised, up-dated and enlarged for the 1980's

ORIEL PRESS
STOCKSFIELD BOSTON HENLEY LONDON

First published 1967
Second edition 1971
Third edition 1978
Twice reprinted
Fourth edition 1979
Reprinted
Fifth edition, revised & enlarged 1980

ISBN 0 85362 187 X

For professional reasons the author writes under a nom-de-plume

Published by
ORIEL PRESS
(Routledge & Kegan Paul Limited)
at
Stocksfield, Northumberland NE43 7NA

Trade enquiries to:
Routledge & Kegan Paul Ltd.
Broadway House
Newtown Road
Henley-on-Thames
Oxon RG9 1EN

Printed by Knight & Forster Limited, Leeds

THIS BOOK

will help you to pass examinations

IN ANY SUBJECT

It is divided into three parts.

PART ONE explains what examinations are, how they are conducted, how they are marked, how to prepare for them and how to pass.

PART TWO helps you to understand why you should be taking examinations and their significance in your life because it is much easier to do anything if you know why you are doing it.

PART THREE is very important. It suggests how you can use opportunities outside the curriculum of school or college to improve your chances of success.

NOTES. Anyone who aspires to the higher levels of education must get used to footnotes. They are comments germane to the subject but to avoid disturbing the flow of ideas they are separated in the form of notes. In this book the notes are at the end. They are indicated thus, *3, in the margin. Please read them.

Examine well your own thoughts.

Chaucer

CONTENTS

PART ONE

Passing examinations is a job to be done. It needs to be tackled in a practical common-sense way. Many failures are not due to lack of ability or knowledge. They are unnecessary.

PART ONE

THE NATURE OF EXAMINATIONS

It is important to approach examinations in the right frame of mind, to have a sensible attitude towards them and get them in a proper proportion to the rest of your life and activities. There is no need to be afraid of examinations yet, every year, there must be thousands of candidates who fail because they panic at some stage. So let us begin by looking at examinations to see what they are and how they work.

EXAMINATIONS ARE A NECESSARY NUISANCE

There are two main reasons for having them. The first is to make people take the trouble to learn. Passing examinations is not the best reason for wanting to learn but really it does help. You might find it more difficult to learn things which you need to know if there were no examinations to work for.

The second reason is to provide evidence that you have reached a certain standard. This is necessary for being able to get, and do, some job or other and it is also necessary if you want to take your education a stage further. This is because, unless you have learned the things the examination is designed to test, you will be wasting you own and your teachers' time trying to do more advanced work. Here again, the examination is partly for **your** benefit. There is no joy in being out of your depth if you can't swim.

But hardly anybody thinks examinations are entirely satisfactory and some of them are being replaced by other methods of testing and selection for education, opportunity or employment. (see p. 34) So far so good, but we still need examinations of many kinds and the object is to pass them.

EXAMINATIONS ARE OF FOUR MAIN KINDS

1. *To test what you know.*
2. *To test your ability to think about and use what you know.*
3. *To test skill or method.*
4. *To test* **you.**

It helps a lot if you know which kind of examination you are taking. Some combine two or more of these kinds but usually there is an obvious emphasis. For example, a medical student's examination in anatomy requires a lot of knowledge of the parts of the body but it also requires some ability to think about how the body works. Without the knowledge the thinking is not much good.

Similarly, a mechanic's trade-test will require knowledge of all parts of an engine and how they work but it may also involve testing the skill of the candidate in taking the engine down and reassembling it.

Ask yourself where the emphasis of the examination lies — in knowledge, in thinking, in skill, or is it a way of finding out about yourself? A good example of the fourth category is the examination which is meant to test the suitablility of your character for a job such as being a teacher, an army officer, an air pilot, a banker, sales manager or a priest.

STANDARD

Some examinations are competitive and your object in these must be to get the highest possible marks. You cannot do better than your best so the important thing is to be at your best (see p. 21)

But most examinations are setting a standard. In nearly all cases it is a very low standard; indeed it is rather frightening to think how many 'qualified' people passed by knowing less than half (insofar as the examination is a valid test of knowledge). Put yourself on the other side of the fence for a moment. If you had been badly injured in an accident would you be happy to think that the hospital doctors and nurses had 'got by' with half marks? (see p. 15) Frighteningly, that is the standard by which we live.

In most of the big public examinations the standard is set by allowing a substantial majority of the candidates to pass so you have to be well below average to fail. It is not a very fearsome standard and, provided that you work fairly hard, organise sensibly, take the examination in a common-sense, practical spirit without any panic, there is really no reason at all why you should fail.

HOW EXAMINATIONS WORK

Examination papers are usually set by people who have some qualification in the subject of examination. They are often teachers or other professional men and women. They are seldom at the top of their profession because examining is boring and not very well paid work. You are not being examined by supermen. Even in university degrees this is generally true.

Often the paper is 'vetted' by a committee or a chief examiner. It is then printed very secretly and sent to the examination centre. The answers which are written by the candidates are called 'scripts'. They are collected and sent to be marked. When there are more scripts than one examiner can mark they are shared out among a number of examiners and care is taken to check that, as far as possible, they all mark to the same standard. This can be done fairly easily with pure *fact* examinations but in other types of examination there could be some variation of standard. Everybody is trying to be absolutely fair but there is a human element in marking. This can be rather reassuring than otherwise! The examination is *not* an infallible system. Its verdict is an *opinion*, not an irrefutable fact.

The examiners who mark papers do so because it is part of their job or because they can earn some extra money or, occasionally, as a professional obligation. In any case it is a boring, tiring job — a chore.

When you sit an examination remember that a weary man or woman may soon be struggling to read your work on a lovely day when it would be much more pleasant to be doing something else. Examiners are human and it pays to make life easy for them by writing clearly and concisely.

PREPARATION FOR EXAMINATIONS

The kind of preparation you do must be suitable for the kind of examination you are going to take, so let us consider the four main kinds of examination separately.

Preparing for Fact Examinations

There is often something rather silly about fact examinations because you may have forgotten most of the facts a week later and it is hard to believe that the effort of learning was worth-while. But in some cases fact examinations are followed by work in which you constantly need the facts and this does make sense. Taking a long cool view, the proper thing is not only to learn the facts but to know permanently where you can get them if you need them. Having known something is, in itself, valuable.

If you must sit a fact examination it's a battle of wits and memory against the examining body. Plan carefully.

1. *Find out what the syllabus really is and don't waste time learning things outside it.*
2. *Look at past examination papers and notice how the questions are spread over the subject.*
3. *Find out the lowest pass mark. Is it 35%, 50%, or do they expect you to get all the answers right?*
4. *If you can't learn the whole syllabus a shrewd look at the spread of questions and the pass standard may tell you what the smallest safe fraction of the syllabus is to secure a pass mark.*
5. *If parts of the syllabus are difficult for you, concentrate on the parts you can do easily. Make quite sure that at least you know these.*
6. *Your object is to learn facts and retain them long enough to pass the examination. You can learn in several ways.*
   - *(a) Visual memory. Write things down and keep on writing them and looking at them.*
   - *(b) Aural memory. Say things aloud.*
   - *(c) Use mnemonics, that is, memory aids, such as rhymes, jingles and key words.*

(d) *Absorption. Keep on reading.*

(e) *Best of all, try to understand the reasons behind the facts. It is much easier to remember what makes sense than something you don't understand.*

(f) *Try to put what you judge you must know for the examination into neat notes which you can revise before the examination and have fresh in your memory. It is better to make your own notes than to buy them ready-made.*

(g) *If you have been badly taught in a subject, or have missed lessons or lectures because of illness, or if you are working on your own, you can buy* 'study aids' *in most of the more common subjects. They are not the best way of learning but they can help you to pass fact examinations. (They can be dangerous for think examinations because the examiner may well recognise the source of your 'thoughts'!)*

7. *Don't get over-tired. It is a battle of wits and memory. You need to be fresh and clear-headed.*

The pure fact examination is educationally suspect but don't forget, your job is to pass the examination, not reform the system. (You may do that later if you pass!) *For a fact exam you cram.*

Think and Fact Examinations

Most examinations require knowledge and to pass them you must have the basic facts. People often make the mistake of thinking that because pure fact examinations are bad educationally they don't need to learn facts.

In preparing for any examination in a subject you should sort out the basic facts and learn them. History is a good example in that you may have an understanding of a period — say, the middle ages — and yet make a nasty mess of the paper because you don't know the sequence of events — the dates. It may be old-fashioned but it is quite easy to learn the lists of facts relevant to a subject such as history or chemistry and it does help if you know them.

Don't be misled by over-idealistic teachers: it is always easier to pass an examination if your thinking has a scaffolding of knowledge.

In this type of examination questions often begin with the word *Discuss* or *Consider*. This is a signal that the examiner wants you the **think,** to give your views about the subject, but don't be led astray. He does not want your *opinion;* he wants a reasoned discussion. To prepare for this kind of examination you must read round the subject, not limit yourself to one book (unless you have a very helpful teacher who makes sure that you discuss all the likely questions under his guidance).

Don't go into the examination expecting to do all your thinking there. You should prepare for the examination by answering questions of this kind so that in the actual examination you are largely repeating work you have done before.

Even so, you may get a surprise question and you need to be able to think. Again mental agility and freshness are vital. *Don't swot right up to the examination.*

Examinations for scholarships, awards and professional appointments are usually intended to test your ability to think about facts.

Skill and Method Examinations

These can be very important and they are a fair kind of examination designed to test what you can do, from playing the piano to doing algebra. According to the subject they can be practicals or written papers and obviously they do test your ability to perform *provided that you let them.* The main obstacle is nervousness. The best way of acquiring the necessary confidence to do yourself justice is to 'know your stuff'. Know that you can do what is required. This means that you have done it successfully before, either in test papers or in test performances. In the case of test performances, especially of music, you can simulate the atmosphere and stress of the actual examination by arranging an audience or getting some distinguished local musician to hear you play the test pieces. Set yourself obstacles and *know* you can overcome them before the actual examination.

This leads us to a digression of some importance to all examinees.

DIGRESSION. Teachers are often very humane and idealistic people. It is their job to encourage, to bring out the best in people, even to make silk purses out of sows' ears as the old saying goes, and often they don't tell their pupils that in real life there are inevitable, inescapable tests of character. For example, a road accident may suddenly present anyone with horribly injured people whose lives may depend upon the responsible behaviour and knowledge of anyone who happens to be present. You may be involved in an accident and see a person you care about die because of your incompetence, squeamishness or lack of knowledge. The happenings of life are not always adjusted for our personal good as they tend to be in school or even in a university. Our quality as men or women is often revealed by outrageous, ugly and obviously unjust happenings and what we do about them.

Don't be too soft about examinations. They do, in a very mild way, test our quality as human beings who can cope with whatever may happen. An examination is a challenge and we should see it as such. There is nothing mysterious about it; there is no reason to get neurotic; it is, in the modern world, one of the challenges we must pass to prove our worth, our sense and our courage. The staunchness and guts of people really do matter and examinations are a very tame way of testing them.

Nervousness in examinations may be partly due to over-preparation, or to lack of a sense of proportion. There is no more excuse for panic in an examination than for panic in serving at tennis when the score is 30—40, match point. But unfortunately the mystique of school assumes courage in sport and not in examinations.

This is partly because parents and others are so silly about examinations and so sensible about sport. In games the success rate is only 50% in each game.

(End of Digression)

Examinations that test You

These begin with intelligence tests, the results of which should not be taken too tragically. 'Intelligence' is a notional assessment which leaves out many of the most valuable qualities of a human being, such as honesty, imagination, initiative, unselfishness and capacity for spiritual or aesthetic experience, but it does have *some* bearing on capacity to pass examinations and to do certain jobs which may lie beyond these examinations.

One way not to fail examinations it to avoid attempting what is beyond your capability. Parents and teachers can be wise advisers but they can also, because of pride, ambition, or a kind of zeal, push boys and girls to attempt the impossible. Most people recognise that for some subjects you have to have special talent. Music, architecture and gymnastics are examples. Most people who are fairly intelligent can pass most subjects up to O Level. After that you really have to look carefully at your own talent and get the best and kindest advice you can: that is the most truthful advice.

EFFECTIVE STUDY

Obviously you must have ability and willingness to learn. You must be prepared to work but to pass examinations you need to work *effectively*.

Study is most effective when you are fresh. If you work at almost anything when you are tired and stale your output will be reduced. This also applies to learning and the input of knowledge. There is no glamour about 'early to bed and early to rise'. It is more impressive to 'burn the midnight oil' but for passing examinations the early hours of the day, when you are fresh and your mind has been resting are the best time for study. *'Early to bed and early to rise'* is old-fashioned but very sound advice.

Learning is a job. It has its own techniques which have to be learned first. Here are some suggestions.

1. Reserve the early hours of the day for study.
2. Work regular hours. If you find a continuous stretch of three hours too much, take a deliberate rest. Divide your time into periods of effective work. This is what school time-tables try to do. In swotting, don't go on and on without breaks or you will be wasting your time on ineffective work.
3. Divide up the work to be done and plan it over the whole period available for study. Make out a time-table and allow for revision periods. Try to keep to your time-table.
4. Don't get over tired in other ways.
5. Keep fit.
6. **DON'T TAKE DRUGS** except possibly under medical supervision. And don't try to 'con' the doctor into prescribing a tranquiliser.
7. Remind yourself that if your work-programme is sensible and you do, say, four or five hours *effective* work each day it is unlikely that you will fail the examination.
8. Most examinations are based on a syllabus. Many candidates don't know what it is! Get a syllabus *and find out all you can about the scope of the examination. Plan accordingly.*

Digests

You can buy 'potted information' books for cramming. They can be useful but it is far better to make your own.

Practise précis writing. Particularly in literary subjects, take each chapter of your text books and reduce it to essentials, say three hundred words. This 'act of concision' is one of the best ways of learning because it makes you think about what is and what is not important. It also provides you with a quick method of revision.

When you have made your précis, type them or write them out very clearly.

Health

The hysterical state into which some people allow themselves to get about examinations is really deplorable. In almost any other situation it would be called FUNK, cowardice, or something similarly unpleasant. In fact it is seldom any of these but it is a state of ill-health one need not get into if one approaches examinations in a sensible way. Parents and teachers, especially of younger candidates, can help, but it is really a personal matter of what sort of person you think you are and how you face up to things.

If you do make yourself mentally sick for an examination you will probably need medical care. This should be available but *it won't pass the examination for you*. Sometimes allowances can be made for illness but this is not possible in most of the big public examinations, and in any case there is nothing gained by being ill. Occasionally degrees are awarded, on a candidate's record, when he has been ill for the examination but it is a misfortune to get an '*aegrotat*' degree, as it is called.

The simple fact is that if you get ill, mentally or physically, you may be unable to take or pass the examination. This is a misfortune against which you should take all reasonable precautions. And don't think there is anything heroic about a breakdown: it is just an awful pity.

Smoking

Smoking is seldom allowed in examinations. Apart from its danger and offensiveness to the growing majority who are not addicted to tobacco it should be avoided by examinees who will have to abstain from their habit during the examination.

The rules that apply to training for sport are just as valid for examinations.

Quack Methods of Learning

There are no subsitutes for study and concentration. These are *not* assisted by background music, tape-recorders under the bed, tranquilisers, stimulants, totems, charms or any similar superstitions. It stands to reason that study should be done in a quiet place with the minimum of distraction. To study effectively in a family room with the 'telly' on is virtually impossible. You may think it is easier because your mind is distracted from your work but you are fooling yourself. Background music is helpful to people doing monotonous, routine jobs in factories because it takes over part of their minds. If you think academic study is like this you really are in trouble!

Parents can help by making sure that you have a quiet, reasonably comfortable place to study, and encouraging you to use it. When this is not possible at home you may be able to get facilities at school, in a library, or at a friend's home.

Pupils in residential schools and students at universities and colleges away from their home town also need a place at home in which to work.

State of mind

Meditation, prayer, spiritual exercises, sport and artistic
*1 experiences, such as performing music, are not to be
despised as ways of achieving calm and confidence. They are not a substitute for study but they can help in preparing for and taking the examination.

Love and Sex

This is a tender and difficult subject but it needs to be mentioned. We are not concerned with the legal, moral or medical aspects except to note that they do exist. The main examination period in people's lives begins about the same time as puberty when young people are changing physically and emotionally. This change imposes a need to adjust one's way of life to the facts of being, in some respects, a different person. Love is perhaps the noblest thing in life. The sex drive to continue the species is tremendously powerful throughout nature. The awakening of love for another person is often, but by no means always, linked to sexual desire and this is not just a problem for young people. It really only ends with death but in the early years when people are trying to find their place in the world and need to study and take examinations if they are to fulfil the twin aims of love and sex, in being able to create a home and rear children, there are many corrupt influences which obscure the natural instincts, which we share with most animals and birds, to preserve chastity until a loving and responsible decision can be made.

It would be idiotic to say 'Don't fall in love' because this is something one cannot help doing, and love can indeed help a candidate in an examination if it engenders a sense of responsibility and indicates objectives.

Co-education has solved some problems and created others, one of them stemming from the fact that girls mature earlier than boys who do not reach their full strength until their twenties, as the sports and athletic records clearly show. The kind of stamina and maturity required of astronauts is achieved at around the age of forty.

For females pregnancy, (even if terminated) and early assumption of the responsibilities of motherhood are serious handicaps to any person who wants to develop her mind by further education, to pass examinations and pursue a career in an occupation which requires qualifications. For males the emotional consequences of premature *2
sexual experience can be serious and the anxieties and responsibilities which inevitably accompany a sexually consummated relationship cannot be other than distracting.

Older people often feel a genuine sadness for young people who are overtaken by the current fashion for being old before their time and certainly, from the point of view of passing examinations, there is much to be said for chastity.

Where a deep, emotional relationship does exist it calls for generosity towards either partner who may be taking examinations. True love, it may be said, should not be demanding or possessive.

Unreasonable examinations

Most examinations are sensible and fair but a few are silly. It is unreasonable, for example, to expect a candidate to create an original work of art, a picture, poem, or musical composition, under examination conditions. If you do have to do this you must not get 'steamed up' about it. Play the system: do the best you can to give them what they want. If there is an element of insincerity that is the examiner's fault, not yours.

Equipment

Long before the examination you *must* find out what equipment you will be allowed or required to take into the examination. This applies particularly to calculators which may or may not be allowed and there may be restrictions on the type of calculator. These can affect the way you prepare for the examination. (Take a spare battery.)

Pen, pencil, pencil-sharpener or knife and rubber are fundamental. Make sure you won't run out of ink. Make sure you have any necessary instruments. It is not fair to yourself, or other candidates, or the invigilator, to want to borrow things during the examination. Most invigilators will not allow it.

In some examinations you are allowed to bring in books, such as dictionaries. Make sure that you have these in advance. Don't rely on getting them from a library the day before.

THE EXAMINATION

Take the previous day off and relax with some distraction to take your mind off the work. Go to bed early. If you *3 have revision notes you may find it helpful to look through them on the morning of the examination.

Get up early, dress comfortably and have a good breakfast.

Allow plenty of time and don't rush.

Check pen, pencil and any materials you will require. (These should have been put ready the night before).

Get to the place of examination before the starting time. Don't be late.

Go to the toilet.

Go to your place as soon as you can and put pen, pencil, instruments, etc., ready.

As soon as you get the script-book or paper read the instructions carefully and comply with them. Fill in your name and any other particulars required as soon as you can. This may save time, and time is precious.

As soon as you get the paper, read it carefully right through. Note particularly the number of questions required, subtract ten minutes from the total time available and divide the remainder by the number of questions. (But see below for compulsory questions).

You MUST attempt the full number of questions. If, for example, four questions must be attempted and you only do two, the maximum mark you can get is 50% even if your answers are perfect. If a question is answered at all, most examiners, especially in literary examinations, will give a few marks and these can make all the difference. One of the main reasons for failure of good candidates in examinations is not answering enough questions.

If a question is COMPULSORY do it first. If you don't do it you will fail. A compulsory question usually gets more marks than the others.

Read each question very carefully and be quite sure what it means; then answer the question. The rule by which the examiner marks is that no matter how good what you do may be it gets no marks at all if it is not in answer to the question, that is, if it is irrelevant. A good example of the kind of mistake that causes perhaps a quarter of all failures is this:-

Q. Explain the consequences of the Dissolution of the Monasteries.

A. A candidate gave a good *account* of the Dissolution of the Monasteries but said nothing about the *consequences* and failed in that question.

ANSWERING THE QUESTIONS

Sometimes questions are in two or three parts and take such a form as '*write brief notes on two of the following . . .*' Remember that if you only answer half the question you can only get a maximum of half marks.

Be very careful to do exactly what the examiner asks you to do. It is useful to pause for a moment and try to see it from the examiner's point of view. What is he actually trying to find out from you? Does it look as though he really wants facts, or does he want your thinking about the facts? Remember that in many subjects, particularly Mathematics and Science, the method may be as important as the answer, that is to say, the examiner wants to know how you think about the subject and the way you work. It depends very much upon the type of examination whether a numerically correct answer is vitally important. It does, of course, help in any case.

Do not use a question as an excuse for writing all you know about a subject. *This is a very common mistake*. A candidate starts off on the right lines and then remembers his notes on the subject and writes down everything without sorting it out. Examiners don't like this and it wastes time — theirs and yours.

Often questions begin with such words as *discuss, explain, evaluate, give a short account of, write brief notes on, consider, compare and contrast, enumerate*. Each of these words or phrases has a different meaning. Pause to think just what the words mean in the context of the question which is asked.

In some questions diagrams are asked for and one could be told to 'explain by means of annotated sketches . . .' or 'draw a map of . . .' This means exactly what it says and if you write an essay instead of producing annotated sketches or a map you may fail, even though you know quite a lot about the subject, because you have NOT ANSWERED THE QUESTION. This may seem very hard but put yourself in the examiner's position. He has to stick to the rules; if he did not it would be very much worse and no-one would know where he stood.

DON'T PAD. The examiner does not enjoy reading a lot of irrelevant material and your 'padding' can actually reduce the marks you would have won for the question if you had not included it. Padding is a waste of precious time.

Write clearly and carefully. In a bunch of badly written scripts the examiner is really pleased to find one he can *4
read without difficulty. He earns his money in perhaps half the time taken for a badly written paper. He may not be allowed consciously to mark down for untidiness and illegibility but it is difficult for him not to be influenced in his marking.

Say what you have to say as shortly and clearly as you can.

In mathematical examinations also, clarity of setting out is valuable and clear figures help you to avoid mistaken reading of your own writing!

Rough work is required in most examinations to be done in the script, often on the left hand pages. Be sure to comply with instructions in this matter.

Don't attempt to crib in any way. The anxiety may retard your own work and if you are caught the penalty may be very serious indeed for your future career. Morals apart, it just is not worth-while.

At all costs you must attempt the required number of questions.

Sometimes a paper is incorrectly printed, most commonly by being blank on one side. This should be obvious. If you do have any doubts about the printing of the paper consult the invigilator at once.

If you finish early go through your answers carefully; you can usually improve them.

In the last ten minutes check quickly through your paper for gross error. If you find you have made a serious mistake add a note to explain that you know you have made it and what you ought to have done even if you cannot correct the answer. Such a note may help quite a lot with a good examiner.

Finally, make sure your script is handed in or collected in the proper way. Scripts can get lost through the carelessness of the candidate.

ORAL EXAMINATIONS AND INTERVIEWS

The oral examination may be simply to test proficiency in speaking a language or a test of ability to read aloud if, for example, you want to be an announcer. But oral examinations can, and are often intended to be a help to the candidate who is not at his best in written papers. In some examinations the oral follows a written paper and is used to raise a candidate's mark but not to lower it. In any case it is an opportunity to be examined face to face with your examiner. Interviews are often supplementary to examinations and are especially important for university admission and, of course, for appointments. The interviewers want to see you at your best. They want to know what you have to offer. Be open with them, not suspicious and don't try to put on an act. They are usually skilful at getting you to talk and this is what they want. The suspicious 'You're not getting anything out of me' attitude is common and unwise in a candidate.

Be polite. Don't be afraid to say 'sir' to the interviewer (but don't overdo it). It is a formal occasion so dress sensibly for it and whatever your views on dress may be remember that your job, for the moment, is to pass the interview and nothing else.

As with all examinations you will do better if you have had a good night's sleep. A haggard, been-travelling-all-night, self-pitying appearance does not help. Indeed self-pity is a very bad gambit all round. A common form of it is 'they never told us at school'. It does not help you to say you have been to a bad school because the interviewers have met many good people who have not had ideal opportunites educationally and yet succeeded. Some interviewers may admire loyalty and despise an attempt to blame the school. Again, it does not help to excuse the lack of qualification by saying 'we could not do it at our school' because most interviewers have met the boy who left school at fifteen, did a full-time job to keep his sick, widowed mother and passed three A Levels by spare time work. (This is true, with many variations, as every experienced interviewer knows).

Interviews are intended to make good the shortcomings of the examination system. They seek to find out mainly what written papers don't reveal. Orals may be meant to help you but interviews are almost always an additional test of suitability for whatever lies beyond them — a course in Fine Art or a job as a psychiatric social worker. An almost inevitable question is 'Why do you want to be..?' Think about this beforehand. It will probably be asked in a roundabout way such as 'What do you actually know about the job of being...?'

BOOKS

Education without books is like cricket without a ball. Despite all the talk about visual aids and modern methods of communication books remain by far the best, cheapest, most accessible means of conveying and storing information and ideas.

You need to have books of your own and by the time you are eleven you should be building up your own library. Put your name in books and treasure them: some will be your friends for life.

In some schools pupils have been led to believe that the school should provide all the necessary books and they are returned to store for other people to use as soon as you have finished with them.

This has been a help to children whose parents can't afford or wont buy books but generally it has discouraged the habit of owning books and this is bad. It might have been better to give help where it was needed and let the beneficiaries keep their books. In some schools and in most colleges and universities students are expected to buy their books and it is part of their education to learn what books to buy.

It is vitally important to study the right books. If there are set books make sure you get these and know them. Don't rely on libraries. If you own a book you can mark and annotate it. This can be very helpful as a method of study and for revision. It is wrong and unfair to mark library books.

Be careful to get good books. Many books are bad and inaccurate. Some are produced for a 'popular market' well below the standard of your examination. Normally teachers in your subject are the most likely to give good advice. Professional bodies and government careers pamphlets are not always up to date, nor are careers books. Libraries do their best but don't just take the advice of a library assistant who finds you a book on your subject. He or she probably knows very little about it but tries to be helpful and can be dangerous. Always look at the date of a book. It is usually printed on the reverse of the title page.

In some subjects you may read a very good, newly published book which seems to contradict your text book. In the examination remember that the examiner may be less up to date than the author, so be careful! Use the book by all means but quote your reference. *'In the recent book by so and so it is shown that . . . etc.'* If you simply write down new information without this precaution you could be marked wrong!

Again, perfectly reputable books may contradict each other. There may be quite different schools of thought in some subjects at the higher levels. Your examiner may be open-minded or he may not. Again be careful: *'while X says so and so, Y contends that . . .'* In an examination it is probably better to be impartial unless you know your examiner as, of course, you may well do in certain types of examination. (See also Part Three page 51).

GRADES

In some examinations, such as the A Level examinations conducted by English universities, grades of pass are awarded, normally from A to E. Concern about grades required for university or college entrance is one of the commonest causes of destructive anxiety in candidates. In part the universities are to blame for this.

Teachers and pupils often ask university departments what levels are required for admission. There is no uniformity between departments or universities. In any one university there may be totally different requirements from department to department. In the more recent foundations especially there is some self-consciousness about standard and heads of department are anxious to establish a reputation. They may try to do this by announcing high entrance standards, such as *'three B's'* or *'a B in the main subject and a C and a D'*. Other departments may distrust A Level results and require only a 'matriculation qualification' which is, in effect, *two E's* but they place great emphasis on school record, head-teacher's report and interview. This may appear to be a much more intelligent approach and such departments or colleges which are looking for people rather than high examination marks, often have the highest academic standards.

There is a very wide choice of colleges and universities and the would-be student is free to shop-around. Most universities know this and welcome enquiries from boys and girls from 16 upwards. If they don't, cross them off your list unless there is a very strong reason for wanting to go there.

Setting a high A Level standard, such as *Three B's*, is a lazy and sometimes even a misleading way of selection because if enough candidates with *Three B's* are not forthcoming the department has to lower its fences or start the session with reduced numbers. No department likes to do this for reasons of pride and, in the long term, self-preservation.

If you want to go to university, polytechnic or other place of higher education go and see the place, talk to students (you are almost always welcome in such circumstances in any Students Union). Make an appointment well in advance with a member of staff. This is normally done by writing to the Secretary of the department you want to enter. Most good departments welcome such enquiries and visits. They make a note of them and often take your initiative into account as a point in favour of admitting you.

If you find that you are not welcome and that admission is purely on examination results, without interview and irrespective of the age at which you take the examination, or whether it's your first or another attempt, you may expect an arrogant and lazy department if and when you go there. You may be wrong but it is not an unreasonable conclusion to come to.

By all means try for the best grades you can get but don't

be too depressed if you don't achieve them and don't believe the dismal counsel of people who say you might as well give up if you can't get *Three C's*.

In a lively department the school record, including extra-mural activities, music, sport, social service etc. will be carefully considered along with the head-teacher's report and you will be interviewed by a panel or a senior member of the staff and much will depend on this. Many university dons remember students with poor entrance examination qualifications who achieved First Class Honours three or four years later. There seems to be little correlation between A Level and final Degree results but any statistics available are vitiated by the policy of departments which only admit the A Level 'cream', so they don't know what the others would have done.

AN ALTERNATIVE TO EXAMINATIONS?

The minds of examinees are sometimes unsettled by criticism of 'the system' and the alternative which is often advocated as being more fair and humane is 'continuous assessment' as it is called. This happens anyway in most schools and shows up in terminal reports. Teachers keep their own records as a basis for advising students and as their own check on examination results. If there are wide discrepancies between records and examination results the school may take this matter up with the examination authority to make sure that a mistake has not been made.

But is continuous assessment really an alternative to examinations, and is it always fair? Continuous assessment, if it were an alternative to examinations, instead of a safeguard, would involve an unpleasant change in the relationship between teacher and student. The teacher would always have an examining role and students would be aware of this whereas with examinations teacher and student are *both* trying to pass the examination! They are on the same side. Furthermore, no matter how scrupulously fair and honest a teacher may be it is impossible not to like some people better than others. There is much to be said for the short, sharp, impersonal examination.

WHAT IF I FAIL?

The fear of failure and its consequences is a common cause of failure. Parents and teachers naturally want to encourage students to do the necessary work but sometimes the spurs which are used do more harm than good. It is far *5 better to encourage regular habits of study and provide the right physical environment than to make a bogey out of failure. The important thing is to acquire a quiet and suitable place of study. Ideally, a study/bedroom is the answer. Adaptations can be made easily, a table can serve as a desk for example, but good lighting and adequate heating are 'musts'. A cold student working in a poor light will be unable to work efficiently.

An important element in this booklet has been the attempt to de-bunk examinations, to show what they are and how they work and encourage candidates to regard them sensibly. In my experience many people who fail examinations do better later on in some other line than they ever would have done in the job for which the examination was required. Examinations can often be taken again and the delay of six months or a year is far less serious than a breakdown.

Examinations are by no means perfect but there is a lot of nonsense talked about them. At the pass standard, with which this booklet is concerned, there is really very little reason indeed why anyone who has the ability to pass should not do so if he is sensible, works reasonably hard and comes to the examination as to a serious game with all his wits about him. Examinations are a necessary test and failure, as it is called, merely means that an opinion has been expressed that the candidate is not up to the standard in that particular activity or subject at the time of the examination. This is a useful thing to know, not a tragedy.

The examination system is imperfect. This is a great consolation. *It would be terrible if it were infallible!*

PART TWO

We are only young once: what are the implications? When you are young you have opportunities to decide what kind of adult you are going to be. Society needs competent and responsible people.

PART TWO

WHY BOTHER?

Some people think that passing examinations is a purely selfish activity. This is not true. We live in a complex society which depends for its standard of living and, indeed, for its survival upon a terrifyingly small number of people whose knowledge, skills, responsibility in management, invention and execution create the jobs which most people take to be their birthright in industrialised countries.

There is a creative minority without whom the rest of people could not live in the way they do. This minority is very different from the aristocracies of former times.

It is now mainly recruited from people who show evidence that they are capable of doing the necessary jobs. One of the most important kinds of evidence is examination results, in the early stages, but experience and performance become more important later on.

Universal and indeed compulsory education in most advanced countries has, in one sense, opened the doors of opportunity to every child but in another sense it seeks to obtain the best talents, regardless of birth, wealth or race, for the benefit of the people, for society as a whole. There has been much political confusion about the purposes of education. Firstly it opens doors of understanding, enjoyable experience and knowledge which give opportunity for a richer life to those who will take the trouble to use the facilities which are made available. Secondly it tries to select those who could benefit themselves and other people by further education and thirdly it seeks to find and exploit for the benefit of society as a whole the creative talents of exceptional people. Modern society needs more talented, skilled and dedicated people and examinations are part of a system (by no means perfect) which enables people to qualify themselves for service.

Higher education is vital to our survival and even to our

comfort. It is quite a hard road, almost a pilgrimage.

But for most people in their teens the goals are more simple and immediate. Few if any can know where they are going or what will be expected of them. The future is uncertain but whatever may lie ahead, habits of responsibility and competence are worth cultivating.

In the 1980's young people are growing up into an over-populated and impoverished world where many millions of people are near to starvation. Whole nations are rich and whole nations are poor, with a few exceptional poor people in the rich places and a few very rich people in some of the poor ones.

This book is addressed to people in the privileged countries and a few lucky people in the poor countries because only they have the opportunity of education leading to examinations which they hope to pass.

A rising standard of living against a background of diminishing resources and higher pay is reflected in inflation. People become more and more expensive to employ if they are to maintain 'the standards to which they are accustomed'. Legislation intended to protect employment has had the effect that such heavy liabilities are placed upon employers as to make them reluctant to undertake the responsibility of employing anyone if they can possibly help it or use a machine instead. Trade unions, protecting their members' interests, establish closed shops which in some cases make entry to a trade almost a hereditary privilege. The professions likewise operate closed shops in the supposed interest of the public.

Nowadays a candidate for employment is asking an employer, whether it be an individual, a company or a public body, to undertake heavy liabilities. Protection of Employment legislation has made it difficult to sack an employee, even for gross inefficiency or dishonesty, so employers, public and private, naturally take great care about appointing anyone and they reasonably require evidence of competence. School reports are distrusted because protection of the individual has made it dangerous for teachers always to tell the whole truth, so the evidence of examination results is required for an increasing number of jobs because having passed an examination is concrete evidence of some ability to do a job properly.

It is becoming less and less easy to get a worthwhile job, or indeed any job, without some tangible evidence of competence.

True, advanced societies now accept responsibility for the unemployed and their dependents but with declining wealth the extent to which this responsiblity can be maintained is in doubt. Opportunities in life depend increasingly upon passing examinations in order to have evidence of competence.

The years of adolescence are, by nature, the years of adaptation from childhood to adult life and education is a part of that process. It is often said that we are only young once and this, of course is true. The opportunities of youth do not come again. It is a difficult and testing time. Many of the old restraints have been removed and this makes it harder. The disciplines which used to be imposed by older *6
people are now commonly the responsibility of young people themselves.

The world needs more better qualified people. Examinations can be a means of 'getting on' but they are also a way of qualifying yourself for service. In the world as it is becoming there is less and less scope for people who have not taken some trouble with their own education. (See also Part Three)

All children are created different and dependent. The ideal education develops personal talents while fitting the individual to take a beneficial place in the community upon which he depends. 'No man' as the philosopher John Donne said, 'is an island. Each is part of the main' (i.e. the mainland of society). The special characteristic of man is that he is an 'improving animal'. Quite apart from the *7 compulsions of evolution man has the *will* to improve. This takes many forms, some of them dangerous and wicked. In this little book we are not concerned with the imposition of ideas upon people: we are considering the process by means of which some people who have talents may find their way to using them for the benefit of mankind.

Snide and envious things are said about the examination system but it is in fact part of a way of improving the human condition by ensuring that people in jobs are capable of measuring up to their responsibilities.

CHOICE OF SUBJECTS

This book has been written on the assumption that you know what examinations you want to take and choice of subject lies outside its immediate scope; but obviously choice of the right subjects does have a bearing on your ability to pass and some candidates do dissipate their energies on too many subjects, or even on the wrong subjects for the career they want to take up.

Most people get good advice from their teachers at school or college and even for boys and girls who think they are certain about their future careers it is wise to take a broad spread of subjects at O Level (or equivalent) so as to keep options open, but also on general educational grounds. Whatever examinations you intend to take in the future you need to be numerate and literate. All too often people who intend to be scientists or technologists forget that they will have to read about, write about and discuss their subject with committees, with clients, employers and so on. They must be able to write and speak well. Candidates on what is often called the arts or humanities side also make the mistake of neglecting knowledge and skills which are necessary in our modern society, and particularly mathematics without some knowledge of which it is impossible to think and communicate about many things which are important in our way of life.

Mathematics is a way of thinking. Likewise the language one uses needs to be studied in its grammar and syntax as well as in the writings of poets and other masters if it is to be effective as a tool for thinking and communication.

Many people, from the age of sixteen onwards, find there are obstacles to doing what they want and, for our present purposes, taking the examinations they want to take, because they have neglected one or other of these two major subjects, mathematics and language, both of which should be precision tools.

But it is at the first stage of advanced examinations (A Levels or equivalent) that choice of subject can be crucial. Often the career you want to take up requires a subject at A Level which is not your *forte*. For example, most sciences, most technologies and some arts, like architecture, require mathematics. Other careers require at least one foreign language. Some require an ancient language.

There is a tendency for teachers to advise people to take their best school subjects at A Level. Quite frankly, and with the greatest respect to the *teachers* concerned, your best school subject may not be your career subject. Many of the most interesting jobs in the world as it is today are unusual, are not covered adequately by careers advisory services and may require a reasonable standard in subjects which are not your best at school. For example you may be very good at English, History or Biology at school but if you really want to be a surgeon you probably ought to take Maths, Physics and Chemistry. In engineering management an aptitude for langauges may be important. In the advanced study of medieval history Latin is essential and Arabic an advantage.

Don't let the aptitudes you have developed at school, sometimes for fortuitous reasons, such as a particularly good teacher in a subject, play too great a part in deciding what you want to do with your life. It may well be that you will have to take subjects you are not good at in order to do what you want. Study for examinations does then become

a means to an end and the passing of the necessary examinations has to be taken very seriously. It is hoped that this book will have helped to establish a technique of taking examinations but it may well be that special coaching will be necessary. This can often be arranged by schools and it is usually wisest to get advice about the best form of coaching or the quality of correspondence courses and
*8 teach-yourself books before making a decision.

Do not rely exclusively on school advice about subjects and don't trust career books entirely: they may be out of date or even wrong. It is *your* career that is at stake. Get the best advice you can and if it is a trade or profession which you want to enter do not be afraid to write to universities, professional institutes, colleges or trade unions for advice. What many aspirants to higher education of all kinds often fail to realise is that good students are hard to get. Universities, for example, are competing for the really talented and keen student. Find out from them how best to qualify yourself.

It is much easier to work for an examination and pass it, even if you are not very good at the subject, if you understand why you are doing it and what it means in your career.

PLAIN OR FANCY?

This question is for boys and girls at school up to the time of deciding what A Level (or equivalent in other countries) to take.

DIGRESSION. Up to 1979 it was commonly thought that the main job of schools was to bring out the latent talents of every child and encourage it to believe that self-fulfilment through the exploitation of whatever inner resources there might be was the proper objective of people in a civilised society.

Milton had written, ‘that one talent which ‘tis death to hide’ in the bitter anguish of his blindness and Gray, in his famous Elegy *had written, ‘Some mute inglorious Milton here may rest . . . .’ Benevolent people have tried, through education, to ensure that there will be no mute inglorious Miltons by providing as far as possible the opportunities for every child to find in itself the creative power of the poet, and a thousand and one other possibilities besides. It was and is a beautiful idea and it should remain a part of education not so much to open doors as to show that there are doors to be opened.*

But education has other purposes already referred to (p 39) and a duty to equip every child as well as possible to find a useful place in the society to which it belongs is being recognised by new emphases in the curriculum. To ‘do your thing’ (no matter how badly) is fine at the recreational level *9
provided that you cultivate other and employable skills. To be employed in ‘your thing’ especially in the arts, and ‘show-biz’ requires outstanding talent because your judge is no mere examiner but a substantial section of public opinion, fickle and swayed by fashion as it is.

In short, education is becoming more realistic, more sensitive to the needs of people who want jobs and the needs of their potential employers. It is becoming more and more obvious that two absolutely basic requirments have to be

*10 *met. They are, firstly the habit of self-discipline and secondly, proficiency in the basic tools of learning and communication which are language and mathematics.*

(End of Digression)

There is a temptation to chose subjects which look interesting or seem to point to a career which you fancy at the time (but you may change your mind). You may be influenced by a teacher whom you like to take his or her subject, or you may under pressure from the school which wants to allocate pupils to subjects according to the availability of teachers. There is also a widespread superstition that biology is good for girls. There is a chronic shortage of good teachers of mathematics and, to a slightly less extent of physics and chemistry. But these three, Maths, Physics and Chemistry, are the basic subjects for all scientists.

The plain basic subjects are:

Group 1. *English* and *Mathematics.*

English is becoming the world language. It has an enormous literature and may have to take precedence over your native language if this is other than English.

Mathematics, as a mode of thinking, logic and communication is fundamental to all the sciences.

For readers of this book papers in all examination subjects are likely to be set in English. Understanding English and being able to write and express your ideas in English is fundamental to all subjects.

Group 2. *History*, *Geography*, *Physics* and *Chemistry.*

These are the basic subjects for trying to understand 'the human condition' in the physcial world.

History is a reservoir of human experience, achieve-

ments and mistakes. It is significant that science 'papers' usually begin with a history of the subject of *11
study. In any human endeavour, to neglect past experience and accumulated knowledge is stupid. History is the discipline of relating present endeavour to accumulated experience.

Geography is about the relationship of Man to the environment in which he lives. Like History it is involved with many other subjects. The pressures of population growth and industrial exploitation of finite natural resources make Geogrpahy a far more important subject than it has been hitherto. It is about the relationship of Man to Nature.

Physics is closely related to Mathematics in that it is not possible to proceed far with the study of physics without mathematical proficiency. But whereas Mathematics is fundamentally a system of thinking, Physics is a means of understanding the way the world is 'designed'.

Chemistry is more intimate than Physics and studies the materials of which the world is made and how they are put together.

Group 3. *Languages*, ancient and modern.

Apart from the obvious usefulness of languages as means of communicating with people who speak languages other than English each has a literature which cannot be entirely acessible unless you know the language. (Translations are always an approximation.) It would be tragic if the languages which enshrine great literature and folk lore were to disappear. Many colleges and universities require examination passes in a language other than English and it is worth noting that this may be one's own language. Schools often assume that 'a modern foreign language' required for university entry must be one of the main European tongues, but if you speak another language at home, it may be one in which you could take examinations.

Classical Latin and Ancient Greek used to be the basis of education in many European countries and each gives access to a rich literary heritage. Much of the English language, especially in scholarly subjects, including Science, uses Greek and Latin words. All modern languages are to some extent fluid, irregular and idiomatic. The advantage of studying classical languages is that they are more orderly, less debased by use and provide the best discipline in grammar and syntax which are applicable to all languages.

If you are really interested in language as such there is much to be said for a Classical education. Conventionally in the West this means Latin and Greek but it could include some oriental languages.

One does not study another language only for the utilitarian reason of being able to talk to the people who can only speak that language. One reason why so many universities require evidence of knowledge of another language is disciplinary — that is to say, it shows that you have begun to learn how to monitor your thinking in your own language by the discipline of thinking in another language.

Fancy Subjects.

One of the aims of education in Comprehensive schools has been to provide the services of teachers in a very wide range of subjects. This may serve the needs of people who are going to discontinue their education in their mid-teens and not proceed to education at an adult level but it provides a forest full of snares for those who do want to go to college or university for what is called 'higher education'.

Such subjects as Archaeology, Art History, British Constitution, Business Studies, Commercial Mathematics, Constitutional Law, Economic and Public Affairs, Geology, Human Biology, Logic, Political Studies, Psychology, Religious Knowledge, Social Biology, Sociology, Statistics, Technical Drawing and Zoology are attractive and may be of considerable value for people who are not proceeding to higher education, and the teachers in these subjects may be very good but if you do want to continue your education in any of these subjects you will almost certainly need to have qualifications in the appropriate basic, plain subjects. So do be careful. It is very disappointing to find that when you have passed examinations the subjects are not acceptable for the courses which you want to enter.

People at universities will probably tell you that what we have called the fancy subjects are better studied when you have a grounding in the basic subjects.

The Great Divide

It is unfortunate that higher education seems to create a division between Arts and Science subjects. This imposes, or appears to impose a career decision at around the age of fifteen for those who want to proceed to higher education but part of the mystique of school is to make you believe that everything is under control. This is not true.

Examinations decide nothing. It is for you to decide and if you have taken the wrong examinations you may have to take more examinations later on. There are now many 'mature students' in Universities, some in their sixties, who have taken examinations normally set for teenagers in order to prepare themselves for entry.

PART THREE

Education does not depend entirely upon teachers and institutions. Awareness, interest in the world around you and a desire to learn are vital. There have never been such opportunities as there are today and many people waste them.

PART THREE

EXTRA-MURAL OPPORTUNITIES

Practically all schools make pupils take tests and examinations as part of the curriculum but many people don't care about passing examinations. They do not see them as being of any real importance in their lives. There are still many jobs which you can get without passing examinations. Some of them are useful and important, but many are routine jobs, some of them on a conveyor belt. Technology is rapidly eliminating these and opportunities for the unskilled are diminishing. Let's leave it at that.

If you do decide to 'improve yourself' which is a rather old-fashioned phrase but accurately descriptive of what people are trying to do when they set themselves to pass examinations, the decision must affect your 'life-style'.

Up to O Level a good school can do most of what is necessary to prepare you for examinations provided that you co-operate, pay attention and do your home-work or 'prep' conscientiously. Even so, some extra effort from you can make a difference.

After O Level and in technical schools, colleges, universities etc., it is assumed that you will contribute to your own education and there are, nowadays, abundant opportunities to do so but they are bound to have an effect on your social and family life. There can be social difficulties for a person who has an objective which requires the passing of examinations. If your father is a rich man whose leisure interests are in expensive recreations, drinks parties and luxurious living you may be even worse off than the son or daughter in a working class family where brothers and sisters are earning 'good money' while you, as a student, are the odd one out. Whatever the social circumstances, from the deprived, single parent home to the millionaire's mansion flat in Mayfair, there are difficulties even for those brought up in what might seem to be the idyllic environment of a cultured middle-class home!

As compared with people who are not working for examinations you have to alter your way of life. You are not snobbish but you simply do not have as much time as other people for whatever activities are customary in your set; and education opens doors of experience and enjoyment which may be closed to others.

Going through these doors is part of the activity of qualifying yourself to be different and therefore able to do jobs which require cultivated minds and skills.

Books are the main source of knowledge and understanding but 'the media' provide a continuous source of information and experience. If you care about football, racing or pop-music, you quickly learn which papers to look at and which radio and television programmes are relevant. If you are aiming in the direction of higher education and 'improving yourself' there is a fantastic richness of opportunity to educate yourself and see programmes, from the production of Shakespeare plays to
*12 series like *Life on Earth*, or *The Great Seasons* and ecological and archaeological studies on a scale of resources and expertise which no specifically educational programme could hope to achieve. Likewise in the arts, it is possible to hear the greatest musical performers of our time — and some of them are the greatest ever — or see living artists at their work, or be conducted by distinguished scholars through public and private collections of works of art all over the world.

Most broadcasting organisations have some commitment to cultural programmes and the demand for these is growing as boredom with stereotyped thrillers and worn out comedy sets in, but the BBC provides for those who are privileged to see or hear its programmes, a unique enrichment of human cultural experience.

If you are a candidate for examinations at any level there is much you can learn, as well as enjoy, by watching *selected* TV or listening to *selected* radio programmes but this does present social problems. You may have to ask for the Royal Shakespeare Company performing Julius Caesar against family preferences for Top of the Pops. Examinations and the culture they represent are divisive. No use pretending they are not.

To be practical: try to see the programmes which are marvellous and sometimes unique opportunities to gain insights into the arts and sciences at the highest levels. Colour TV in your own private room is ideal; otherwise try to persuade your family (if they are not already convinced) that they might enjoy what you want to see and hear.

There are also specifically educational programmes, such as those provided by the Open University in Britain which are presented with visual resources which no school or other university could rival.

If you habitually watch programmes presented by the leading scholars of our time, as you can do several times a week, and if you attend to theatrical, musical, ballet and opera performances you cannot help but absorb knowledge, ideas and experience which will be helpful to you in examinations over a wide range of subjects. Much of what you will see and hear is produced to a very high standard and that, in the end, is what examinations are about.

There is also the news. Much of it is sensationalised but it is necessary, if you are qualifying yourself for a responsible skilled job, to know what is going on and be able to think about it. By its nature the TV presentation of news is limited and newspapers which you can read at whatever time suits you, are in many ways preferable. You can select what interests you whereas radio and television tend to process you.

Newspapers cater for a variety of tastes and can be more specialised than broadcasting. Many are aimed far below the O Level standard. If you want newspapers to help you in the process of passing examinations choose those which carry, as regular features, book reviews and articles on science, industry, economics and the arts.

Interviews and oral examinations are, as we have seen, a very important part of the system. You can't prepare yourself overnight. You need to have acquired the habit of keeping in touch with current thought and affairs. If you are aiming at a particular trade or profession remember that almost every trade and profession has its own journals. If you want a job in publishing or bookselling, for example, read *The Bookseller;* it will certainly help you with your interview and likewise with other jobs which have their own journal.

But let us have a word of warning about learning from 'the media'. Don't believe everything you read, see or hear. Supplement and check by reference to books. Try to assess the intellectual level of what is offered. Popularisation often means over-simplification and as anyone who has worked in that medium will tell you, television is inevitably superficial, seeming to cover an enormous amount in, say half an hour, but it is much better for demonstrating than explaining. Some subjects, like biology and crafts are particularly suitable but other very important subjects like philosophy and economics are not.

Learning requires concentration and it follows that reading, listening and viewing should be selective. I sympathise with people who keep the telly on all day as a defence against the neighbours' noise machines. But a constant background of telly or radio develops habits of inattention which are bad for people and very bad indeed for those who want to study for examinations. For you as an examinee it is best to select your programme and then treat it with the same degree of attention as you give to a lecture, making notes if necessary.

SPEECH

Finally I want to say a word about speech. It would be a sad loss if all the dialects disappeared. If you are brought up to speak a dialect by all means be proud of it and there is no need to be ashamed of a north-country or west-country or any other accent BUT many boys and girls acquire slovenly, inarticulate ways of speaking and there are often group pressures to conform to these mutilated forms of speech sometimes punctuated with swear words or clichés. If you feel it is socially necessary to speak in this way among your friends you must become bi-lingual and learn to speak properly when you want to do so.

Language is one of the great achievements of mankind, the medium of poetry, drama and most forms of thinking and communication. If you speak badly it is difficult to think well because much (not all) thinking is done in words. Apart from this there are many jobs which necessitate clear, precise speaking. As English becomes more and more a world language it is necessary to speak English in a way which can be understood by anyone who has learned English whatever his nationality.

When you go for an interview or oral examination you will be severely handicapped if you cannot speak clearly and express what you want to say naturally and without embarassment. TV and radio provide many opportunities to listen to people speaking well but don't expect to do so
without some trouble. You can learn by listening but the *13
art of speaking well needs to be cultivated and what you learn in the English classes at school is relevant to the way you speak. Some people are shocked when they hear themselves on a tape recorder — they may have good reason to be.

'OVER THE FENCE THE GRASS IS GREENER'

It is often said that many great men would never have got through the modern examination system to reach their eminent positions. There is a grain of truth in this but that is about all. Such evidence as we have suggests that most eminences would have passed examinations easily if they had had to do so. Indeed, they might have found them easier than the devious, chancy, often very unfair and sometimes dangerous methods by which they did have to advance.

The modern examination is often seen as a fence beyond which stretches a lush and rewarding career if only, by hook or by crook, the examination can be passed; and the examination is regarded as an arbitrary, unnecessary barrier. In fact it gets harder. One is often very sorry for the person who, by fantastic hard work or good luck, passes an examination he should have failed. Take the example of the boy who wants to be a doctor. He must have three A Levels. If he can't pass these it really would be very difficult indeed for him to pass the long succession of more difficult examinations in the medical student's course.

It is also thought that examinations at lower levels have very little to do with 'the real job' such as being a medical student and then a doctor. In fact the sheer drudgery and hard work involved in most professions is not easily realised by people who want to enter them. One needs to be able, and one has to prove one is able, to settle down to long unpleasant jobs and the learning of a great deal of dreary information.

Don't think an examination is a barrier between you and paradise! In many ways it is harder on the other side. The examination is not a once for all do-or-die occasion. You are more likely to pass if you realise that you have to take it in your stride.

EXAMINATIONS IN PERSPECTIVE

Taking examinations is part of a process of growing up and developing yourself. Examinations are not an end in themselves. Passing is a creditable thing to do but it does *14
not mean you are a better person. It does mean you are qualified in what the examination was intended to test, and that you are prepared for continuing your education or putting your skill into practice. Our modern kinds of society could not survive without people who have passed examinations and in the process you have probably made it possible for you, yourself to live more fully.

This is partly because of the opportunities which qualifications give you but more because of the doors which have been opened and the insights gained in the course of your education.

One last point: if you have not had a chance to study, if your home background has been difficult or unsympathetic, if you have been set-back by illness in the family or by being sick yourself, or if you have taken a wrong turning, remember that thousands of people have overcome initial difficulties of this kind and it is now easier than it ever was to get help in improving your education whatever age you may be. You need initiative and a willingness to work. You can only find these in yourself but if you do have them the 'system' nowadays is far more helpful than it ever was before.

Finally, there is bound to be an element of luck in examinations so, to you who have read this book I would say that I hope it has helped and —

GOOD FORTUNE!

NOTES

Note 1

It should be noted that while music is a valuable activity, playing in a group may involve a great deal of work and with folk and pop groups this often extends beyond midnight. This kind of exacting activity is a common cause of strain, inattention and failure.

Note 2

The teaching of human biology and sex instruction in schools generally focuses upon the physical aspects of sex thus making the relationship of man and woman seem far more simple than it really is. You don't begin to know the full story until you have reared a family which is the natural and fundamental purpose of intercourse.

Note 3

A long walk in the country is ideal. Schools should encourage and facilitate a day off before the examination.

Note 4

One of the reasons why girls often excel boys in examinations is that they generally write better.

Note 5

I would not encourage parents to offer bribes — a new bicycle, a tape-recorder, that kind of thing. It betrays a wrong attitude, an excessive anxiety and, after all, it is the candidate who is going to gain in the end by passing the examination. A celebration afterwards is a different matter.

Note 6

Lack of parental guidance and moral restraint gives young people a great deal of freedom to make mistakes some of which impose lasting restraints upon freedom.

Morality is a serious matter which has concerned mankind since before the dawn of civilisation. People who are brought up with a moral code are lucky. They may change or reject it later but life is very much easier and potentially more successful if you can accept, without worrying, a proven pattern of life. Anyway, don't try to put the world (or even your own family) to rights when you are trying to pass examinations. Many people do so without realising how much they are sacrificing.

Note 7

So far as we can tell other species do not consciously seek to improve by change. The idea of man as 'an improving animal' is discussed in *Civilization, the Next Stage* by Bruce Allsopp (Newcastle, 1965, 1971, Tokyo 1976)

Note 8

Many coaches, courses and aids are ethical: some are not. Take reputable advice otherwise you may not only be wasting money but actually diminishing your examination prospects. One of the disadvantages of using pre-packed learning in the form of revision aids is that examiners may recognise the answers and in *think* examinations this is damaging.

Note 9

Insofar as education encourages people to believe that the world owes them a living in what they fancy they would like to do it is doing a disservice both to pupils and the community. It is not the job of educators to foster self-centredness and selfishness.

Note 10

Self-discipline is difficult and has to be learned, most usually by accepting an established well-tried discipline. The discipline of school is a good beginning and should be welcomed.

Note 11

The term *papers* used here is the normal description of the form in which scientific research is presented to learned societies and professional scientific journals.

Note 12

The Great Seasons, David Bellamy, 1981. (BBC in association with Oriel Press)

Note 13

The phrase 'the Queen's English' is a literal description of the standard set. One can hardly do better than listen to the British royal family.

Note 14

Being a better person depends upon qualities of character which examinations cannot test. Qualifications improve your potentiality for good and for evil.